James Alston

James is an actor and writer from Gloucestershire, now based in London. He studied at the University of Exeter, where his journey as a writer began, writing short plays for student radio. He later trained as an actor at the Guildford School of Acting.

He has written two short films: *The Ex* (as co-writer, 2017, EspectroMX Films) and *House Party* (for The House Is Now Open, 2020, OSO Arts Centre). In 2020, he co-wrote *A Cratchit Christmas Carol* for the stage, which was produced by Get Out Of My Space.

Scarlet Sunday is James' debut play as a solo playwright.

First published in the UK in 2024 by Aurora Metro Publications Ltd.

Based at Books on the Rise, 80 Hill Rise, Richmond, TW10 6UB UK

www.aurorametro.com   info@aurorametro.com

FB/AuroraMetroBooks Twitter/X @aurorametro
Instagram aurora_metro

With many thanks to: Inês Almeida, Aisha Khan

Printed in the UK by 4edge printers on sustainably resourced paper.

ISBNs:

(print) 978-1-911501-24-4

(ebook) 978-1-911501-25-1

SCARLET SUNDAY

by

JAMES ALSTON

AURORA METRO BOOKS

CONTENTS

OMNIBUS THEATRE

Omnibus Theatre is a multi-award-winning independent theatre in Clapham, South London. Finalist in the Fringe Theatre of the Year 2020 and 2023 The Stage Awards, Off-West End Award winner 2018 and 2020, and recipient of the Peter Brook/Royal Court Theatre Support Award in 2016. The heart of the organisation's ambitious programme lies in classics re-imagined, modern revivals and new writing. Omnibus Theatre also provides a platform for LGBTQ+ work, aims to give voice to the underrepresented and challenge perceptions. Since opening in 2013, notable in-house productions include *Woyzeck* (2013), *Macbeth* (2014), *Colour* (2015), *Mule* (2016), *Spring Offensive* (2017), *Zeraffa Giraffa* (2017), *Queens of Sheba* (2019), *The Little Prince* (2019), RICE! (2021), *The Human Connection* (2021), *The Girl Who Was Very Good At Lying* (2021), FIJI (2022), SAD (2022), DRUM (2022), *The Woman Who Turned into a Tree* (2023) and *Compositor E* (2023).

Omnibus Theatre is led by Artistic Director Marie McCarthy and Executive Director Bridget Kalloushi. Patrons include Dame Judi Dench, Sir Lord Michael Cashman, Paulette Randall MBE and Rikki Beadle- Blair MBE

ASLANT

Aslant Theatre Company is an international female-led collective producing new work and imaginative adaptations of the classical repertoire. We provide a platform for re-telling and remembering the stories of the past using an eclectic and provocative range of practices.

Aslant was founded by creative producer Antonia Georgieva (she/her) in 2019, with the company's Offie-nominated debut production MUSE premiering at Camden People's Theatre and enjoying a successful extended run at Tristan Bates Theatre (now The Actor's Theatre). Director Aida Rocci (she/her) later joined the company introducing a slate of projects centring on translation and international work, including the upcoming UK premiere of Oscar nominee Cristina Comencini's hit play Two Rounds (Due Partite).

The company has previously been supported by UK and international funding bodies and partners including the Arts Council England, Jerwood Arts, Jermyn Street Theatre, Istituto Italiano di Cultura, the Bulgarian National Culture Fund, Enfi Teatro, Teatro Il Parioli among others.

We are storytellers:

We believe that storytelling should and does infuse every aspect of our lives. That is why we are conscious of who gets to speak and tell stories. All history is told with a particular slant We aim to give a voice to those who are or have been historically "aslant" and in particular we champion the stories of women past and present.

We are interdisciplinary collaborators:

Our work is eclectic and works towards pushing the boundaries of the theatrical form through interdisciplinary approaches. We don't just make plays. We operate on the boundaries and bring different forms together.

We are educators:

A significant strand of our work aims to equip both performance makers and people from other walks of life with relevant and transferrable skills that will unlock their potential and encourage them to share their stories.

We are Aslant:

We are constantly asking ourselves how we can flip the dominant narratives, tell the untold stories of the past, examine the overlooked points of view, and retell the classics in a different way.

Facebook: /AslantTheatre

Instagram: @AslantTheatre

X: @AslantTheatre

https://www.aslanttheatre.com/

BIOGRAPHIES

Camilla Aiko – AVA

Camilla graduated from Bristol Old Vic and theatre.Credits include *New Plays: Japan* at The Royal Court. Screen credits include feature film *Lee* opposite Kate Winslet and Andea Riseborough, *Doctor Who* and Amazon series *Fifteen Love*.

Sorcha Kennedy – YASMIN

Theatre: *UNION* (Arcola Theatre), *Contractions* (Omnibus Theatre), *Rainer* (Arcola Theatre), *Diary of a Somebody* (Seven Dials Playhouse), *Sam Wanamaker Festiva*l (Shakespeare's Globe), *Humbug!* (Citizens Theatre, Glasgow).

Radio: *The Nazis: Road to Power* (BBC Radio 4), *Whenever I Get Blown Up...*(BBC Radio Scotland).

Nominated for Lead Performance - Offie Awards 2022 (*Rainer*, Arcola Theatre). Sorcha trained at the Royal Conservatoire of Scotland. She is a filmmaker and visual artist. Her debut short, *Sisyphos*, starring Leonie Benesch, was selected for various BAFTA & Oscar-qualifying film festivals.

Imy Wyatt Corner - Director

Imy trained on the Drama Directing MA at Bristol Old Vic Theatre School.

Direction includes *The Last One* (Arcola Theatre), *Passing* (Park Theatre), *Duck* (Arcola Theatre, Jermyn Street Theatre), *Beasts* (Edinburgh Fringe), *Humane* (Pleasance Theatre), *Snail* (Vault Festival), *Gaslight* (Playground Theatre), *Baby, What Blessings* (Theatre503, Bunker

Theatre), *Walk Swiftly & With Purpose* (Theatre503, North Wall Arts Centre) and *Happy Yet?* (International Theatre, Frankfurt)

Assistant / Associate direction includes *Private Lives* (West End), *Relatively Speaking* (UK tour), *The Dance of Death* (UK tour), *Love All* (Jermyn street theatre), *Troilus & Cressida* (Redgrave Theatre) and *The Straw Chair* (Finborough Theatre)

She was a Creative Associate at Jermyn st Theatre 2022/3 and is currently an Associate at Arcola Theatre.

Antonia Georgieva - Producer

Antonia Georgieva is a creative producer with experience across theatre and media in the UK, the US, and Europe. She is particularly passionate about interdisciplinary performance that engages audiences in novel ways. Her work has been supported by the Arts Council England, Jerwood Arts, the European Cultural Foundation, and Goethe Institute. She was a Creative Associate at Jermyn Street Theatre in 2023/2024.

Recent credits include: *Two Rounds* (Jermyn Street Theatre), *How We Begin* (VAULT Festival), work.txt (Soho Theatre), *The Last Sunset* (immersive), *KITCHEN* (immersive).

Acknowledgements:

Thank you to Bluey Little, Madeleine Allardice, Eoin McAndrew, and Imy Wyatt Corner, whose notes, dramaturgy, and support on earlier drafts were so essential to the development of this play.

Thank you to Antonia Georgieva and Aslant Theatre for bringing this production to the stage. Thank you to Arts Council England for financially supporting the project.

Thank you to Marie McCarthy, Sam Pout, and the entire Omnibus Theatre team for all their support and belief in the play.

Finally, thank you to my partner Abby, for all her love and support.

SCARLET SUNDAY

James Alston

Presented by Aslant Theatre Company, *Scarlet Sunday* was first performed on the 28th February 2024 at The Omnibus Theatre, London, with the following cast and creative team:

<u>CAST</u>
Camilla Aiko – AVA
Sorcha Kennedy – YASMIN

<u>CREATIVE TEAM</u>
James Alston – Playwright
Imy Wyatt Corner – Director
Cat Fuller – Set & Costume Designer
Catja Hamilton – Lighting Designer
Odinn Orn Hilmarsson – Sound Designer & Composer
Ibraheem Hamirani – Stage Manager
Antonia Georgieva – Producer
Frederick Zennor – Associate Producer
Sam Pout – Dramaturg

SCARLET SUNDAY

James Alston

Characters:

AVA   A writer, mid-late twenties.

YASMIN   An arts journalist and gallery curator. Early thirties.

Note: Content warning. This play contains descriptions of domestic abuse.

SCENE 1

A café somewhere in a city. It is summer, amid the hottest days of the year.

A young woman, AVA, sits alone at a table for two.

Birdsong can be heard, as if deep in the country.

After a moment, YASMIN enters, carrying two coffees.

The birdsong fades.

YASMIN   Sorry!

She places the coffees down at the table, and sits opposite AVA.

YASMIN   The queue was a nightmare.

AVA   Don't worry about it.

YASMIN Everyone getting their iced lattes!

AVA I don't blame them.

YASMIN Oh, sorry, did you want one?

AVA Er –

YASMIN If you've changed your mind I can get you one.

AVA No, no, of course not.

YASMIN You sure? I really don't mind.

AVA It's very kind of you but I'm okay, thank you.

YASMIN You're sure?

AVA Absolutely.

YASMIN Fair enough, if you're sure. It would probably take me another half an hour anyway, wouldn't it? Do you want mine? I haven't drunk out of it or anything.

AVA I'm really fine.

YASMIN Okay, okay.

AVA Thank you.

YASMIN Not at all. Thank *you* for meeting me.

AVA It's okay.

YASMIN It is hot though. Don't you think so?

AVA It is.

YASMIN Hot hot hot. Scorchio. The Dog Days.

AVA Pardon?

YASMIN This time of year, something to do with the Dog Star. Days hot enough to drive dogs mad. I don't know why I know that but there you go. Useless fact of the day!

AVA   No, it's – I never knew that.

YASMIN   Makes you want to be a kid again, I always think, when it's this hot. When you could just jump in a paddling pool, or have water fights! I wish it was socially acceptable to have impromptu water fights. Did you ever do that? Water fights and things?

AVA   Not really, no.

YASMIN   You didn't? Oh my god Ava, you missed out!

AVA   We didn't really have any of those things – water fights, paddling pools, we didn't have them.

YASMIN   What a deprived childhood!

AVA   You come here a lot, do you?

YASMIN   Hm? Oh. Yes, "my local". Really cool place isn't it? Just down the road from the gallery, you see. They do excellent iced lattes here. It is roasting. Regretting not getting the iced latte now? Next time, just say "Yasmin, don't get me a bloody extra hot americano, gimme the iced latte with extra ice." That's what you need. I'm just teasing don't worry.

AVA   It's okay.

YASMIN   Hotter here than in the countryside I suppose?

AVA   Sorry?

YASMIN   That's where the house is, isn't it? Out in the sticks, no?

AVA   Oh, yes.

YASMIN   Yeah. Hotter here, is what I was saying.

AVA   Is it?

YASMIN   I think so? I've heard that. The concrete just absorbs heat and radiates it. No trees to cool it down.

All those exhaust fumes, making the air thicker. Like being in a big oven.

In the countryside you've got – well, you've got trees, fields, rivers.

AVA That's it, nothing but trees, fields, and rivers.

YASMIN You know what I mean – Fresh air! It's just better, isn't it?

AVA This is your favourite coffee shop?

YASMIN I suppose it is, yes. People are nice, they do good coffee here.

AVA Coffee's alright – so you were saying, about the countryside?

YASMIN I don't know... I could quite see myself out there. One day. It's exciting here, but it is so crowded, and dirty – just *people*, you know? Love people of course, well you've got to, right?

But out there, there are no distractions, no noise. Here there's everything, but out there – there's nothing.

AVA That depends on what you mean by nothing.

YASMIN Yes. Mmmm. Yes. Thank you again, so much, for coming out here.

AVA S'fine.

YASMIN Was it a long journey?

AVA Not really. Twenty minute drive to the nearest village with a station. Hour train from there, so.

YASMIN Oh that's not bad! Trains are handy aren't they? When they're running of course – when they're not all on strike! No, but good for them, though, good for them. But also – AAARRGH!

AVA That's why I drive now, mostly. Not very eco, I know, but what do they expect when they make them – trains – so expensive, and they're never running anyway nowadays. What do they expect us to do? I'm sorry, if you want me to comment on strikes, politics, anything like that is off the table, I'm afraid.

YASMIN Oh no – it's nothing like that, don't worry! I'm not that kind of writer.

AVA You're not?

YASMIN No.

AVA I have to be careful. Hope I didn't offend.

YASMIN Oh! Totally fine.

AVA Good. I sort of see why you like it.

YASMIN What?

AVA The coffee shop. It's nice, it *is* nice. But it's very busy.

YASMIN It's popular, because it's a good coffee shop. People like it. I should say – if it even needs to be said – I was very sorry for your loss.

AVA Yes.

YASMIN It's a loss to the whole world.

AVA That's what people have been saying.

YASMIN Because it's true.

AVA Yeah.

YASMIN I'm sorry, I just wanted to say. Because otherwise – you know?

AVA Yeah.

YASMIN It's hard. God. Being there in the house now, I

can only imagine. There must be so many memories.

AVA   Yes.

YASMIN   I had a Grandpa. He died. Grandma stayed in the house on her own for years. I hated visiting that house. Sorry, Ava, I am looking at that steaming cup of coffee that you've got, on this scorching hot day, and I really think you'd be a lot cooler and a lot happier with an iced latte – may I get you an iced latte?

AVA   Um.

YASMIN   Their iced lattes really are excellent – the secret, I think, is the huge quantity of sugar.

AVA   Fine, yeah, um, thank you. That would be – that would be nice.

YASMIN   Fab. Any kind of milk?

AVA   Moo milk please.

YASMIN   No problem, back in a sec. Wait.

AVA   What?

YASMIN   What kind of milk did you say?

AVA   Just – just normal cow's milk please.

YASMIN   Right. Just, I think you said something else.

AVA   No.

YASMIN   Okay. It's just you sort of did though?

AVA   What did I say?

YASMIN   It sounded like –

AVA   Oh no / Moo milk?

YASMIN   Moo milk?

YASMIN   Yes, "moo milk".

AVA   Sorry, I wasn't really –

YASMIN   It's fine, it's fine! But what is it, it's cute, what is it?

AVA   It's a stupid childhood thing.

YASMIN   I think there's a story.

AVA   Really isn't.

YASMIN   Shouldn't have said it if you didn't want to tell the story! Where's it from?

AVA   Why do you want to know?

YASMIN   It's fun, isn't it?

AVA   Is this really relevant?

YASMIN   Don't know yet. Come on, if you tell me, I'll stop going on about it.

AVA   I – really? You actually want to know? When I was little that's what I used to call milk. Normal milk.

YASMIN   Adorable. Why?

AVA   I think it was because I found it amazing that milk came from cows. I just couldn't get my head round it. See, it's weird!

YASMIN   But you were a kid. And kids are weird.

AVA   Yeah, well, I hope it was useful to you.

YASMIN   It's a funny story! This will make you feel better. When I was a child my favourite things in the world were these little tubs of strawberry trifle that my mum would get me sometimes as a treat. Incredible! They had – you know, they're in layers – you had your cream, your custard, the sponge, then the jelly and strawberries and all that goodness down at the bottom. Anyway, when I asked for it, I would always call it

"Jelly Hiding"! "Can I have Jelly Hiding, Mum?" Get it?

AVA   No?

YASMIN   No!? The jelly was *hiding*, Ava! Underneath the sponge and the custard, it was *hiding!*

AVA   Right, I get it.

YASMIN   So, there, you're not alone.

AVA   Mine's definitely more embarrassing.

YASMIN   Kid stuff. Everyone has weird kid stuff.

AVA   God, I could still devour those little trifles. Would be dangerous though because I've outgrown them. I'd need to eat like four of them in one go to feel full.

Have you got something like that? Like, a real comfort food from childhood that still gives you that warm feeling inside?

AVA   Oh, I don't know…

YASMIN   Come on, you must have one?

AVA   Guess I don't remember.

YASMIN   Really? No food memory at all that brings you joy?

AVA   Again, don't see how it's relevant.

YASMIN   So you do have one!

AVA   Well…

YASMIN   Come on.

AVA   I've already told you one story.

YASMIN   Yes and it was great! I promise I will shut up about food after this.

AVA I'll hold you to that.

YASMIN Here we go.

AVA It's not exciting.

YASMIN So?

AVA Well...I used to love buttered toast.

YASMIN Oh my god, yes.

AVA You know, good thick bread. Loads of butter, melting and seeping into all the little holes.

YASMIN And it's got to be real butter right? Not having any margarine here.

AVA Oh no, real butter.

YASMIN And it's got to be salted of course.

AVA Of course.

YASMIN Oh god, yeah, hot buttered toast. Good choice.

AVA Yeah. Food of the Gods.

YASMIN Absolutely.

AVA Dad would make it for us. I mean, me and Rowan, my –

YASMIN – your sister.

AVA Of course you know of her.

YASMIN She's hardly off our screens.

AVA Tell me about it. When we weren't feeling well that's what he would make. He must have had some magic or something because he made that buttered toast taste like the best thing ever.

YASMIN   It's so fascinating.

AVA   Is it?

YASMIN   Yeah, it is, I'm not being sarcastic. We only ever got to know one side of him. The man you knew, Ray Blackwood the father, he's a mystery to me.

I was going to get you a drink. Sorry, I'll do that now.

AVA   It's okay. Don't worry about the coffee.

YASMIN   Oh?

AVA   Yeah. Thank you, but I'm not thirsty.

YASMIN   That's fine. That's okay.

AVA   This is a very strange interview.

YASMIN   Sorry?

AVA   I thought you wanted to do an interview. That's what you contacted me about?

YASMIN   Well. Yes, that's what I was driving at.

AVA   But we've just been talking about the weather, and milk, and trifles, and toast, and – iced lattes. I'm just – sorry – I'm just – what is this?

YASMIN   Well, I wanted to try and ease into it.

AVA   But we've just been talking about – about nothing. Just weird small talk and I don't really know what I'm doing here.

YASMIN   I'm sorry, Ava, it's just my process. I like to get to know the people who I'm meeting, so that we can get a sense of each other. Build a rapport, and trust. Trust is very important.

AVA   You got that from buttered toast?

YASMIN   This is just a first step to decide whether this is a collaboration we want to pursue together; and I do see it as a collaboration. Because I want to write about the real Ray Blackwood. The man you knew. Like I said, you knew him better than anyone alive. I'm interested in that.

Pause.

AVA So, who are you, Yasmin? You work at the gallery, but you are a journalist as well?

YASMIN I am a curator of modern art. I also write an online arts column.

AVA You blog.

YASMIN I – it's an online arts column – but I suppose a "blog" is – it's very popular. I do know my stuff, don't worry. I'm not a tabloid hack.

AVA You keep busy.

YASMIN I don't know how to keep still, my wife is always telling me that.

AVA Mmm. I read a few of your articles.

YASMIN Doing a bit of research?

AVA Well, I don't come out to meet just anyone.

YASMIN That's very sensible. Lots of weirdos out there. What did you think of my work?

AVA Yeah, good.

YASMIN That bad?

AVA I thought they were insightful. Thorough. Interesting.

YASMIN I sense there's a "but" coming.

AVA Well...

YASMIN   I'm sure worse has been said in the past. I've got thick skin, go on.

AVA   I had a lot of thoughts about one in particular.

YASMIN   Which one?

AVA   Oh, it was your piece entitled: "Most Instagramable Galleries in the UK".

YASMIN   Oh. Well – that's –

AVA   Can you remember which one got the top spot?

YASMIN   You might have to jog my memory.

AVA   Tate Modern of course: just head straight in, post a picture of the Turbine Hall, in and out in five minutes, don't even need to bother with the exhibitions – I'm paraphrasing, of course, but that's the gist.

YASMIN   That was –

AVA   From a curator of modern art no less.

YASMIN   Right, okay...

AVA   Do you see why I might be slightly concerned?

YASMIN   Yes – I do, but –

AVA   You did ask me what I thought.

YASMIN   I did, yes, I did do that.

AVA   I just thought – if we're going to work together, I should know the person who will be interpreting my words.

YASMIN   Quite right too. But if I may –

AVA   So, is that what interests you? Giving your readers the inside story of which galleries were best to take a selfie in?

YASMIN   No, it's not.

AVA   Because there were others too: "Best Galleries in London to Take a First Date" – lots of insightful journalism there – and my personal favourite "Top 10 Artists with the Most Tragic Backstories *brackets* Number Three Will Shock You *close brackets*".

YASMIN   Now hang on – If I may, I wrote those articles years ago, I've grown a lot since then. That kind of stuff, it's clickbait of course but that's what you need to do to stand out on the internet. And that audience – I think I'm more suited to a different kind of readership.

AVA   A better readership?

YASMIN   Not *better*. No. I have a great respect for my readers. But, *you know*. This piece, it's not going to be anything like those kinds of articles. I'm not interested in sensationalism, I'm interested in facts.

AVA   Great, fine, you don't need me for that. You can look at his paintings in a gallery and you can read the hundreds of tedious articles and essays that have been written about them and I can go back home.

YASMIN   I don't want to just focus on the paintings themselves, I want to write about the man behind them. The greatest artist of our age and we don't know that much about him. Who was he?

AVA   Just like every other journalist prying into my father's life, my family, looking for the next front page.

YASMIN   I want a story, yes. Something big, yes. I want something raw, yes. Bloody, yes. But not sensationalist, *sensational*. And I'm not a journalist, I'm an arts writer.

AVA   If you say so.

YASMIN   I'm not after anything cheap. I want real

truth.

AVA   You sound like him.

YASMIN   He understood what real truth was. The truth that I'm looking for, I think you could be the key to unlocking it. So, who is Ava Blackwood? I know nothing about her.

AVA   You want to write about my Dad, so why do you need me?

YASMIN   You're a part of his story, and the next best thing to talking to the man himself. What's your passion, Ava?

AVA   I'm a writer.

YASMIN   Anything I would have –?

AVA   Nothing you would have read, no. I use a pseudonym anyway, so you wouldn't know it, even if you had.

YASMIN   What do you write then?

AVA   Short stories mainly. I have a couple of collections published.

YASMIN   So you're a storyteller. Like me.

Ava, I'm not afraid to say this plainly, but despite what you think you know about me, I'm a fucking good writer. And as a writer, one thing I am very, very good at is writing the truth.

If we do this, you'll be entrusting me with your story, and I understand the value of that – I do. And whatever that truth is, whatever story is inside of you, you can rely on me to tell it truthfully.

AVA   How do I believe you?

YASMIN Because if all I wanted was something cheap, sensationalist, viral, you are not the Blackwood sister I would be speaking to right now. No offence.

I would be speaking to Rowan. She's the star. Everyone knows her face, her name. Great clickbait. No one has a clue who you are, I'm sorry.

But you are important, and you and I can create some incredible work together.

AVA You think that, do you? You think that you could bring me here, buy me a coffee, talk about buttered toast, and I would bear my soul to you.

YASMIN No, that's not –

AVA I think we're done here. I should go.

YASMIN Oh, listen, I'm sorry –

AVA Thank you for the coffee –

AVA goes to leave.

YASMIN Ava, Ava, please just wait.

AVA Goodbye, Yasmin, it was nice to meet you.

YASMIN Wait until I say what I have to say and then you can go if you still want to but just hear me out.

AVA I've heard enough.

YASMIN Your father's story –

AVA Yes, yes, I know, the man behind the paintings, I'm not interested.

YASMIN Yes, but there's a particular story, I think it's the key to understanding him, his work, everything –

AVA I wish you luck but I can't be part of this.

YASMIN *Scarlet Sunday.*

Pause.

AVA   What?

YASMIN   I know.

AVA   *Scarlet Sunday*?

YASMIN   Yes. Yeah, I know, it's niche.

AVA   Why – *why* that?

YASMIN   Some people think it was just your father trying to wind us art critics up, teasing us. But I think *Scarlet Sunday* was a final masterpiece that your father was driving towards his whole career but never fully realised, and that's fascinating to me. What could that say about him as a man? Let alone as an artist?

But he only ever spoke of it cryptically, never confirmed or denied anything, and now we can never know. Except maybe we can, because you're here. You grew up with him, Ava.

If anyone is going to know anything about the truth of *Scarlet Sunday* then it is going to be you. I understand that I am asking a lot. It's your father's story, your story too. All I can do is promise that I will treat it with the greatest care and respect.

Whatever the truth of *Scarlet Sunday* is, it's important to me. Of course, if it's not for you then I respect that. It's been an honour just to meet you.

There is silence for a moment.

Then, AVA takes out some paper and writes something down.

AVA   You said you drive?

YASMIN   I do, yes.

AVA gives the slip of paper to YASMIN.

AVA   This is my address. Meet me here next Friday at eleven.

YASMIN   You want to see me again?

AVA *(pointedly)* Yes. You're not busy, are you?

YASMIN   No! No, I'm free as a bird... But at your house? I'm more than happy to meet somewhere like this if that'd be more comfortable for you?

AVA   No, it has to be there.

YASMIN   Why's that?

AVA   How else would you see it?

YASMIN   See what?

AVA   *Scarlet Sunday.*

Birdsong.

SCENE 2

The days turn. Another hot, bright day in summer. Ray Blackwood's studio.

The attic of a large house in the middle of nowhere. This is a room that has hardly been touched in months, if not years. It is dusty and still.

There is one door leading off to the rest of the house. In one corner, amongst some clutter, nearly hidden, a canvas covered with a dust sheet.

The room sits, waits. Birdsong.

The voices of AVA and YASMIN can be heard from elsewhere in the house.

YASMIN *(Off)* Hold on, I need a moment.

AVA *(Off)* Alright.

YASMIN *(Off)* Three, two, one. Okay, I'm ready.

AVA *(Off)* Okay.

The door opens and YASMIN steps in, followed by AVA.

YASMIN Wow. This is the place!

AVA Yep.

YASMIN Where it all happened.

AVA All of it.

YASMIN I can't believe it. I'm standing in Ray Blackwood's studio. This is pretty special. Thank you, Ava.

AVA Don't thank me yet.

YASMIN No, but – inviting me here, to your house, to his space. I don't take it lightly.

AVA I'm sorry that it's so stuffy. All the heat sort of rises and collects in here I think.

YASMIN You can't really escape it on a day like today – I swear there's no wind at all!

AVA I suppose you should make yourself at home?

YASMIN At home? This isn't a home, this is a chapel, a cathedral.

AVA If you say so.

YASMIN This is how he left it?

AVA You're the first person, apart from me, who's been in here since he died. Not even Rowan's been in here.

YASMIN I'm honoured. To tell you the truth, I was quite surprised when you invited me.

AVA Surprised?

YASMIN I don't like to admit defeat, but I was pretty sure I'd lost you for a moment last week.

AVA Let's just say you caught my interest.

YASMIN I do tend to grow on people.

Ava, I have been able to think of little else but this for the past week! God it's like it's infected me. I am so bloody excited.

AVA Excited?

YASMIN Yes! I mean – I don't know if you have a sense of just how significant this is. People have been speculating about what *Scarlet Sunday* is or was for years.

AVA I know that people had theories.

YASMIN A lot of people thought it was just a myth. I'm going to make so many academics cry.

AVA I didn't really pay much attention to that side of things. I know Dad was very happy to have all the speculation flying about.

YASMIN Course he was, he loved to mess us around. But it's made me think... an article's not enough. I think this could be a book.

AVA A book?

YASMIN Yeah!

AVA Why?

YASMIN Because the implications of this piece may rewrite our entire understanding of your father's work!

That needs a book. I don't think I'd struggle to find a publisher. This could be earth-shattering. So...

AVA So?

YASMIN So.

AVA So?

YASMIN Where's this special painting?

AVA Oh.

YASMIN Hold on! Wait. It's not – it's not the room is it?

AVA The room?

YASMIN His final masterpiece – the culmination – *Scarlet Sunday* is the *studio* itself?

AVA Ah – well –

YASMIN Is that what's going on? That would be *so* Blackwood, going all Tracey Emin right at the end. Is that what's happening?

AVA No, it's not the room.

YASMIN Oh!

AVA There is a painting, an actual painting.

YASMIN Got you. Got you. Sorry! Got a bit over-excited! So, where is it?

AVA It's not out at the moment, it's packed away.

YASMIN Oh. Okay! And we'll be having a look in a bit, yeah?

AVA Sure, later. So it's a book. Telling my story?

YASMIN Yes. The whole story of *Scarlet Sunday* and your father – which includes you.

Don't worry, nothing like "10 Most Instagramable Galleries", or whatever it was. A proper book.

AVA   But it was such a compelling read!

YASMIN   Alright, yeah, they were a bit naff, but be fair; I wrote those articles when I was barely out of university. You couldn't have read my more recent work could you?

AVA   I did.

YASMIN   Oh. And?

AVA   Do we really want to go there?

YASMIN   Oh god. What?

AVA   It's fine, look, you're here. I invited you here. We're good – I hope. We don't need to –

YASMIN   No, no, I've got to know now.

AVA   Do you?

YASMIN   Yes, yes, I do. It will bother me otherwise.

AVA   Well...

YASMIN   Come on, I can take it.

AVA   You got upset last time.

YASMIN   I didn't.

AVA   You were annoyed, I could tell.

YASMIN   I can take it! Honestly.

AVA   I read your piece about the place for art galleries in the modern age.

YASMIN   Yes. Go on, what's wrong with that one?

AVA   I didn't think it was bad.

YASMIN   No?

AVA   No, it was very... articulate, passionate, forceful even.

YASMIN *(with a drip of sarcasm)* Oh, you flatterer.

AVA   But –

YASMIN But?

AVA   But that's just it, it felt too passionate, too forceful, when at the end of the day we are just talking about galleries. I mean, there're wars going on.

YASMIN But I am an arts writer. I could talk about how the world's falling apart, but at the end of the day art is what I'm paid to write about.

AVA   Just an observation.

YASMIN No, it's – you're right, probably. Someday I'm going to dig out one of your early short stories and give you a little review. Payback.

AVA   I'd like to see you try to find them, I use a pseudonym, remember.

YASMIN Shit. Very smart. Maybe I should have done that, saved myself the trouble of having my back catalogue dragged into the light of day.

AVA   Alright, I might have been a bit harsh. To be fair, a lot of your recent stuff I thought was good.

YASMIN Are you trying to save my pride?

AVA   No, I'm being genuine.

YASMIN An example?

AVA   Well, the one that really stood out to me was your piece on Picasso.

YASMIN Oh? I like that one too.

AVA   I found your comments on his legacy very interesting, considering that he was – you know – a violent misogynist.

YASMIN   He was a very complicated man. But artists are, aren't they? Not all of them are perfect.

AVA   Putting it mildly.

YASMIN   I can disapprove of everything Picasso was as a man, but his art speaks for itself.

AVA   You believe that do you?

YASMIN   Absolutely. Art takes on its own life in the eyes of the beholder. But I'm not a huge fan of Picasso. It's like, "Yes, weird 2D horses and women with triangular breasts are great but it doesn't touch my soul." Your father on the other hand, he was on another level altogether.

AVA   High praise.

YASMIN   He's the best. How else would you describe him? I can't think of an artist that compares within the last few decades.

AVA   The artists that are coming up after him are clearly influenced by the Blackwood style. He originated an entirely new movement!

Until someone else comes along and captures the imagination of the world. Then they'll be the new "thing".

YASMIN   If they do, then it will only be because of the foundations he laid. His prolific output alone is enough to justify his status; in his "Red Years" he produced more masterpieces than Picasso, Van Gogh, Rothko! As his daughter I'm surprised you're so sceptical.

AVA   Maybe I'm too close to it?

YASMIN   Well, what about the Foundation! The Blackwood Foundation – all that charity work, the mentorship of young artists; he was in schools, hospitals, you name it, spreading the power of art. He did so much good.

AVA   It's funny though.

YASMIN   Funny?

AVA   Well, speaking as someone who actually knew him, he hated the outside world. Hated socialising. Didn't particularly like people in general, come to think of it. Why do you think he brought us out to the middle of nowhere?

YASMIN   Like I said: artists are full of contradictions.

AVA   Doesn't it make you wonder, though? Why? Why do all that when the reality was so different?

YASMIN   This is why I'm talking to you. You can tell me all about the real Ray Blackwood.

AVA   Ah yes, tell my side of the story.

YASMIN   Exactly.

AVA   The problem I have is, and don't take it the wrong way, but your lot – academics, writers – you all talk loftily about how "powerful" his art is, how "revolutionary" he was. But it's all just theory, where's the *truth* that he cared about so much?

YASMIN   What do you mean?

AVA   Show me somebody, a real person, who was profoundly *moved* by his art.

YASMIN   I can speak from personal experience.

AVA   Can you?

YASMIN Yeah. The first painting of his that I saw changed my life.

AVA Which one?

YASMIN *Tears.*

AVA *Tears?*

YASMIN I was at uni. Art History, second year. I was on the verge of packing it all in, if I'm honest; the course, the career I had planned, everything.

Not to be too much of a cliché but it was a time of change for me. I was learning things about myself. Who I was, what I liked, who I liked.

Looking back I am so glad because I was finally discovering "me". But at the time it led to me feeling, I don't know, untethered from who I thought I was, and what I thought I wanted. One day I took a visit to the gallery, just to clear my head. Maybe get inspired again? And that's when I saw it for the first time.

What was strange was that in that moment everything else sort of fell away. The sounds around me, the other paintings, they just dissolved. It was – It was like finding someone who breathed the same way as you.

AVA I didn't take you for someone who'd be into that hippy stuff.

YASMIN Hippy stuff?

AVA Yeah. Sounds like the sort of thing Dad would say, "the breath of life in art".

YASMIN Alright. Yeah, it's silly.

AVA No... it's not... I didn't mean – I get it.

YASMIN Art just does something to our brains. There's a reason why we've been making it since the caves. It gave me the tether I needed. I think I owe my whole life as it is now to that moment.

AVA   Your whole life?

YASMIN   Yes, my job, my writing, my marriage even.

AVA   Oh yes, your wife.

YASMIN   Natalie, is her name.

AVA   Are you happy?

YASMIN   Well, I haven't married anyone else!

AVA   She's your special someone, the one the makes your heart beat?

YASMIN   That's her.

AVA   Just you and Natalie then? No one else. No children?

YASMIN   Just us.

AVA   Do you want children?

YASMIN   Wow, now we're getting into it.

AVA   Well, do you?

YASMIN   I – I think we do. When the time is right. At the moment, we're – then we have to decide how we'd go about it, what's right for us? I don't know.

AVA   But children are very much on the horizon, at some point, somehow.

YASMIN   Yeah. You see, Nat's always wanted a boy. A little boy that she can mother and mollycoddle.

AVA   But not you?

YASMIN   Well, no, of course I'd love a boy. But I've always thought – whenever I've pictured my child it's always a girl.

AVA   Your little girl. Love her. Please.

YASMIN   That's parenting 101, isn't it? Gotta love them, if nothing else.

AVA   I'm serious.

Beat.

YASMIN   Well, thank you for the advice. Anyway, we're not here to talk about my family.

AVA   But you're so keen to learn all about mine.

YASMIN   Yours is far more interesting. And now...

AVA   Yes?

YASMIN   May I see the painting?

AVA   We were having a nice chat, weren't we?

YASMIN   We can continue having nice chats. But I would really, really like to see *Scarlet Sunday*.

AVA   Like I said, it's packed away.

YASMIN   Yes. It's packed away. Oh, Ava, you've got to satisfy my curiosity somehow then. I am, in case you hadn't guessed a colossal geek. I need something to geek out on! Like, there are theories:

AVA   About *Scarlet Sunday*.

YASMIN   No, not just about *Scarlet Sunday*. There's been a lot of speculation by those of us – fans, academics – who study your father's work, that he used you, his daughters, as models.

AVA   Dad used us for his work, yes.

YASMIN   I knew it! Sorry – it might seem dumb but I've got a bet on with someone at work and you've just made me fifty quid richer.

AVA is taken aback by this news, but YASMIN doesn't notice.

YASMIN Which ones are you in?

AVA Between Rowan and I, practically all his best.

YASMIN Wow. *Little Girl Lost*?

AVA Yes. That's me.

YASMIN *Picnic on the Edge*?

AVA That was Rowan.

YASMIN This is so interesting. *Juno Ascending*?

AVA Me again.

YASMIN *Tears*?

AVA Rowan.

YASMIN Never together?

AVA Never together except for one piece.

YASMIN And which one was that?

AVA *Scarlet Sunday.*

YASMIN Now that is interesting. The only one you're both in?

AVA Yes.

YASMIN So, it's one of a kind. Of course, now this is not why we're here today, not at all, but... you know, worth thinking about, Ava. Talk about "cash in the attic".

AVA I'm not sure I could sell it.

YASMIN No, no, of course. Sentimental value, completely get that. But if you *did* decide to sell it, you know, you could make some serious money. You wouldn't believe the power of provenance. My friend

Siobhan, she works at Christie's and last year they hosted an auction for an original first edition of a *The Mr Men* book.

AVA What?

YASMIN Yep, kids' book. Up for auction.

AVA *The Mr Men?*

YASMIN Guess how much it went for?

AVA Couple of grand?

YASMIN Higher.

AVA Ten k?

YASMIN Higher.

AVA Higher?? Er, twenty?

YASMIN Higher!

AVA Fifty??

YASMIN One hundred thousand. *The Mr Men.*

AVA What? You're joking.

YASMIN Nope. Isn't that mad?

AVA Which Mr Man was it?

YASMIN Which one?

AVA Yeah, in the book.

YASMIN Oh, the main one, I suppose? The protagonist.

AVA I don't think there is a protagonist in *The Mr Men.*

YASMIN What about the first one? Hold on: (*She takes out her phone and Googles "Who was the first Mr Man?"*) Mr Tickle apparently.

AVA Of course.

YASMIN   So there you go. But you're not selling it so forget I said anything. But if you were, if that was a path you decided to go down, you know, I could help with that, as well. I know people in the business, I know how the game works. I could be really useful.

AVA You had a bet.

YASMIN   Sorry?

AVA   You said you had a bet on with someone.

YASMIN   Oh yeah, just a silly bet with a friend – well, I say friend more like "frenemy". He thought that the theory that you and Rowan are in the paintings was a load of rubbish. I disagreed, so we decided to bet on it. And I won, can't wait to see the look on his face.

AVA   Does he know about this meeting?

YASMIN   What?

AVA   Does he know about *Scarlet Sunday?*

YASMIN   Ava - ?

AVA   I'm serious, did you tell him anything?

YASMIN   No, no I didn't tell him anything.

AVA   Then how would you have proven it?

YASMIN   I don't know what you mean.

AVA   You had bet with him that Rowan and I are in the paintings. But if he didn't know you were coming here today, speaking to me, if he didn't know that then how were you going to prove it?

YASMIN   No, it was more like – if one of us could... find the most compelling evidence, that sort of thing. It wouldn't make sense for him to agree to the bet if he knew I was speaking to you, would it? I've fleeced him really, I suppose. Deserves it.

YASMIN   It was just a silly bet, for fun.

AVA   Does anyone else know?

YASMIN   I'm not sure I –

AVA   Just tell me the truth, please.

YASMIN   No one.

AVA   Are you sure?

YASMIN   Well...I did tell Natalie. But she's my wife, I tell her everything.

AVA   And will she tell anyone? Can you trust her?

YASMIN   Excuse me?

AVA   Yasmin, can you trust her?

YASMIN   What is that? Yes. Yes, I can trust her, I would trust her with my life. What's the matter?

AVA   I can't have – I don't want to attract the attention of the whole world. If you knew what it was like after he died... press, and fans, and all sorts crawling all over this place like ants. While I'm going through – and people are knocking on my door twenty times a day, watching the house from the road, following me –

Rowan has people to insulate her from that kind of thing. I have no one.

YASMIN   I haven't told anyone, and I won't. This is the biggest story of my career so far. I'm not going to take any risks. You can trust me. But, I have to ask, are you being completely open with me?

AVA   What?

YASMIN   Ava –

AVA   You think that I'm lying?

YASMIN   I'm just concerned –

AVA   You think I'm a liar.

YASMIN   I don't.

AVA   Sounds like it to me.

YASMIN   It's a question of trust.

AVA   Why would I lie to you?

YASMIN   You heavily implied that you were going to show *Scarlet Sunday* to me – that's why I came.

AVA   I said I'll show you later.

YASMIN   Why not now?

AVA   You couldn't possibly understand.

YASMIN   Ava, why am I here?

AVA   I don't have to prove anything to you.

YASMIN   There are other people who I could be talking to about your father.

AVA   Who? Oh. Ice Queen? Rowan! Good luck, she'll never talk to you.

YASMIN   I was in contact with her agent recently and they said that they thought she would be open to a meeting, under the right conditions.

AVA   Yes, the condition that you don't ask her anything about our so-called childhood! She won't – God, it's hot – she won't tell you anything, not the things that I know/

YASMIN   What does that mean?/

AVA   Are you not boiling?

YASMIN   What did you mean by that?

AVA   She won't tell you anything about *Scarlet Sunday!*

YASMIN   Neither are you. Currently. I just need to know that it's here.

YASMIN moves towards the piles of clutter, looking for some sort of sign of where the painting is. Maybe: "It must be here somewhere?"; "Here? Here?"

At some point YASMIN gets too close to the real 'Scarlet Sunday', and AVA winces or in some other way reacts that gives YASMIN a clue.

YASMIN   There? It's been staring me in the face the whole time. Why don't we go over there and take a look?

AVA   No.

YASMIN   Ava.

AVA   I can't do that.

YASMIN   We can do it together.

AVA   I can't – I don't want to.

YASMIN   Just a little peak.

AVA   It's too much.

YASMIN   Come on, a little peak can't hurt can it?

AVA   Stop it –

YASMIN   You want to really.

AVA   I said no!

YASMIN   Okay.

AVA   Stop it, don't do that.

YASMIN   Okay, okay, I'm sorry.

AVA   I don't want to.

YASMIN   Ava, what's wrong?

AVA   Doesn't matter.

YASMIN   Ava, it's just a painting.

AVA   You couldn't possibly understand.

YASMIN   I could try. You could help me to understand.

AVA   Do you think that objects can be haunted?

YASMIN   Haunted?

AVA   Or paintings, specifically.

YASMIN   No, of course I don't.

AVA   Why not?

YASMIN   Because – because ghosts, hauntings, they don't exist. They're made up.

AVA   What about people, can they be haunted?

YASMIN   What has this got to do with *Scarlet Sunday?*

AVA   You said it yourself, art takes on a life of its own in the mind of the beholder. And if the painting is in your mind, then so is whatever's in the painting. You've let it in. And maybe it can climb out of the frame.

YASMIN   The eyes of the beholder.

AVA   What?

YASMIN   I said the eyes of the beholder, not the mind. You misquoted me.

AVA   They say that eyes are the windows of the soul, the mind. Perhaps they're doors too?

YASMIN Are you saying that you think *Scarlet Sunday* is haunted?

AVA No, of course I'm not, that would be ridiculous. I'm trying to explain why I don't think you should be in such a hurry to look at it. There are consequences.

YASMIN Ava, if you're worried about what the painting depicts, you don't need to be. I've studied your father's work for years, I know how strong – unsettling – it can be. I can handle it.

AVA You have no idea.

YASMIN You don't have to look at it, but if it's okay with you, I'm going to go and have a look now.

AVA No.

YASMIN It's okay, I'm sure I've seen a lot worse.

AVA No, it's not –

YASMIN Now I think is the time.

AVA You don't understand!

YASMIN I am trained to handle paintings, I know what I'm doing, it'll be safe.

AVA Don't touch it!

YASMIN Then please! You have got to tell me! What is it? What is it about *Scarlet Sunday?*

AVA You won't understand.

YASMIN So you keep saying. But you won't help me to understand, you won't tell me plainly why you are so terrified of me going near that painting. Ava? What is going on? Right... I'm sorry.

AVA What?

YASMIN   I think I've come as far as I can here.

AVA   You're going?

YASMIN   I don't want to do this but I can't keep going round in circles.

AVA   Great, just leave me in – you really are just going to walk away?

YASMIN   I told you, I came here for *Scarlet Sunday*, I came here for a story but to be honest, Ava, I feel like I've been a made a fool.

AVA   You don't want to know about Scarlet Sunday?

YASMIN   I'm not sure I believe there is such a thing, Ava.

AVA   Well, maybe this whole meeting was a mistake.

YASMIN   Yeah I think you might be right there.

AVA   Goodbye.

YASMIN   I'll show myself out.

YASMIN goes to leave.

AVA   Shit. No! Yasmin!

YASMIN   Goodbye, Ava.

AVA   Don't leave me alone.

YASMIN   I'm sorry, this was a bad idea.

AVA   Please, I apologise, I wasn't – shit – Yasmin, stay, just for a bit please, please – don't go - !

AVA grabs YASMIN in a desperate attempt to stop her from leaving. YASMIN immediately wheels round, shocked.

YASMIN   What are you doing?

AVA   Oh –

YASMIN   Don't touch me!

AVA   I'm I'm sorry – I don't know what I was –

YASMIN   Don't do that.

AVA   – it's the heat, I can't think - you can't go, not yet.

YASMIN   This isn't – I don't want this.

AVA   No, please, I'm sorry, I – it's his secret!

YASMIN stops.

YASMIN   What?

AVA   *Scarlet Sunday* is his secret.

YASMIN   Yes, his secret painting hidden for years.

AVA   Not the painting, what it represents. His secret. Mine too.

YASMIN   I don't want to be messed around.

AVA   I'll tell you. I'll tell you everything. Just stay, please.

YASMIN comes back into the space, with her back to AVA she takes out her phone and starts to record a voice memo.

YASMIN   Go on.

AVA   We were home-schooled, until the age of sixteen, did you know?

YASMIN   I know that he was…unconventional. Not the biggest fan of the education establishment.

AVA   He thought it stifled creativity.

YASMIN   "School is the death of creative thought." Yes, can't say I fully agree with him, can't say I fully disagree with him.

AVA   What better way to prove his point than by demonstrating it with his own two girls.

YASMIN   How did that work out?

AVA   He was a lousy teacher, never had time for it. He was more interested in spending time in his studio. He didn't have many rules in the house, but there was one that we were not to break under any circumstances: don't go into Dad's studio.

I can remember my seventh birthday – ours, Rowan and I are twins, you know – I can remember it with amazing clarity. That was the birthday just before Dad's career really took off.

YASMIN   The beginning of his 'Red Years'.

AVA   That day, I remember he actually made a bit of an effort. He made a big breakfast, there were probably heaps of buttered toast. We had birthday cake – for breakfast! And why not? No school, no teachers, just us and Dad. But Rowan, she – well, she got a bit hyper, a bit worked up. We were playing, and I seem to remember that, somehow, I lost her.

I looked everywhere. All over the garden, down by the stream, the woods, no sign. I looked in the house, I looked in every room, no sign.

There was just one room I didn't look in. I found her here. The one place we weren't supposed to go. And she had trashed the place, like a bomb had gone off.

Suddenly, Dad is there, and then there's shouting, and crying, and before I know it – I still remember the sound. Like a soft thump.

YASMIN   What?

AVA   That is my earliest memory.

YASMIN   Oh my God.

AVA   Rowan was crying, then I started crying – and you know what he did? Our father? He threw us out of the studio, shut himself in, and he went to work. Hours, days passed and at the end he had a brand new painting –

YASMIN   *Tears.* The painting that made his name. I suppose…it's not uncommon, is it? Some people's idea of – of discipline – it's –

AVA   It was a bit more than that. He started taking Rowan into the studio alone with him.

"Rowan is going to come and help me paint now," he'd say. I'd have to go and play outside on my own until they were finished. They'd be hours.

When Rowan came out she'd have these… marks… on her body and her face – If I asked her about them she wouldn't talk to me. And if I asked Dad, all he would say is that she "got them while playing" and that I wasn't to worry. I just accepted it.

YASMIN   You were a child.

AVA   And all I could think of was "why doesn't he want to play with me? Why doesn't he love me?" I was so envious, I didn't notice the new paintings coming out of the studio, I didn't notice Dad's name appearing in bigger and bigger galleries. All I cared about was when he was going to pick me.

I used to pray to God, to the Fairy Godmother, Father Christmas, that he'd pick me one day.

YASMIN   But…you did model for him. You said.

AVA   My wish came true. There's an old dog kennel near the front drive. He took me down there in the middle of winter, no coat, no warm clothes, and he locked me in there overnight. No food, no warmth, no water.

"What did you see, little Ava? What did you see in the dark?" He asked me that as he ran me a bath and made me hot buttered toast.

That's when he began using me regularly.

YASMIN   "Using you"?

AVA   We were his tools.

YASMIN   You – you modelled for him, you inspired him –

AVA   He used us! For his *process*.

YASMIN   I can't –

AVA   His own children.

YASMIN   I feel sick.

AVA   Do you? I'm sorry, would you prefer to hear about how he blended colour? Would you prefer to hear about his charity work? Well that story's been told already.

YASMIN   Hurting children?

AVA   Eight years of my life. The period you all call his "Red Years".

YASMIN *(more to herself than AVA)* Please... please...

AVA   His most prolific era.

YASMIN   ...please not him too...

AVA   What?

YASMIN   ...it's so, so stuffy, I feel –

AVA   Are you listening to me?

YASMIN   I am – yes, I am.

AVA   I'm saying that it was the last one. *Scarlet Sunday*.

AVA goes toward the covered sheet in the corner.

AVA   We were fifteen then. I remember the day was hot, boiling hot. Still and airless.

It began the same way it always did, except this time he asked for both of us.

And after he did what he wanted to do, he didn't ask for us ever again. He didn't need us anymore.

I could always hear the birds outside, when he was doing it. I started focussing on that sound to take my mind away.

Now it's all I can hear. Birdsong.

After some time, a beat or a protracted silence, whatever feels right:

AVA   Say something.

YASMIN   This...this is a trap, isn't it?

AVA   A trap?

YASMIN   You're saying these things to manipulate me.

AVA   Why would I do that?

YASMIN   I – I don't know! I have no idea.

AVA   Then how can you accuse me?

YASMIN   Because I don't know you, Ava. I have hardly any idea who you are! But him, I – I have followed him and his work for years! I've soaked myself in it! And now you're tainting it all.

AVA	That doesn't make my story any less true, and you know it, you just don't want to admit it to yourself.

YASMIN	It's – he isn't – wasn't, he wasn't about that – listen, couldn't you open a window or – it's not *him!* It's not the Blackwood I know.

AVA	But you don't know him, Yasmin! You never met him!

YASMIN	He was – as an artist he was all about truth, and beauty and –

AVA	And pain. His medium was pain. Come on, Yasmin, you're not stupid. You've seen his paintings, you know what they depict.

YASMIN	Artistic expression!

AVA	You yourself brought up the theory that we were his "models" – it was an open secret! Did no one ever put two and two together?

YASMIN	He had his demons, he admitted that. But *children?* His own children?

AVA	Yes!

YASMIN	But he loved children! He was always trying to help children. The Foundation did so much amazing work with children, some of them victims of abuse themselves!

AVA	Yes. He helped hundreds of children across the country and the world. He also abused his own. Both statements are true.

YASMIN	But, I – I... I loved him. It feels heavy now. Sitting inside of me. Dark, and cold. And rotting. Festering. Poisoning... God, how I loved him...

AVA	What you loved was a lie, a myth. It was never

real. But I, standing here, I'm real. My body that bore witness is real. It's all true.

And even if it burns me from the inside out, even if it burns you too, and this whole world, it will never stop being true. Look at me. You know it, don't you?

YASMIN   It's all ash now. This whole time, years of my life, it was just... Fuck. Fuck. Fuck. Fucking – fucking bastard!! I'm sorry, I'm sorry, I'm so so sorry!

AVA   You believe me?

YASMIN   I do. I do, I promise. Forgive me. But it's over now. He can't hurt you anymore.

AVA   Before he died I stayed with him, I cared for him... isn't that strange?

YASMIN   He was your father.

AVA   I stayed here. And he died, and I'm still here, and now he comes to me, in my dreams, he comes to me again and again and I wake up and I'm here in this... this fucking house! And I cannot breathe with that thing in here with me.

YASMIN   Why don't you move out?

AVA   I can't, not yet.

YASMIN   Why? What's stopping you?

AVA   It needs to be gone.

YASMIN   What?

AVA   *Scarlet Sunday*... it... this can't go on! It can't go on or I'm just going to die, I'm going to suffocate! It – it has to be destroyed.

YASMIN   Destroyed?

AVA   Yes, I want to be free.

YASMIN   Okay –

AVA   I don't want to see him anymore. I don't want to be trapped here anymore.

YASMIN   And you think this will help?

AVA   It has to! But I need you to do it.

YASMIN   Me? Why does it need to be me?

AVA   I wouldn't ask if it wasn't the only option I had.

YASMIN   …You can't do it, can you? You've tried, but you can't.

AVA   Look, if you're worried about – I actually own it now. I own the house, I own everything within it, that was what I got after he – so I can do with it whatever I want can't I? Please, Yasmin. I know I can trust you, you're a good person. Please help me.

YASMIN   Okay.

AVA   You're with me?

YASMIN   I'm with you.

AVA   Thank you. We're doing this then?!

YASMIN   We're doing it!

AVA   We're doing it!

YASMIN   How – how are we doing it?

AVA   Burn it.

YASMIN   Shit.

AVA   Has to be – remove all trace – we need – I don't know where my matches are.

YASMIN   I have a lighter?

AVA   Will that be enough?

YASMIN   I don't know – you think something else? Like a lighter fuel?

AVA   Alcohol? I have a bottle of nasty cheap gin downstairs?

YASMIN   That'll do!?

AVA   Surely!

YASMIN   Yeah!

AVA   You're with me?

YASMIN   Right behind you!

AVA exits, YASMIN follows but then hesitates. She looks back at the studio, the enormity of what she has learned lands on her – it all means something different now.

She looks over at the canvas – 'Scarlet Sunday', still covered. She hesitates... a thought crosses her mind. She takes hold of the sheet covering the canvas – lifts it... and gasps in horror and awe at what she sees. Birdsong.

The door opens and AVA rushes in, carrying a bottle of cheap nasty gin – the sight of YASMIN gazing, transfixed, at the painting stops her in her tracks.

AVA   Yasmin? – What are you doing?

YASMIN starts, drops the sheet back over the canvas.

YASMIN   Ava.

AVA   What are you doing??

YASMIN   Ava.

AVA   You weren't supposed to look at it!

YASMIN   Ava, I'm, I'm, I'm –

AVA   Sorry? I don't want to hear it.

YASMIN   I know, I know, I just needed, I needed to see it once, just once, just to know, just to see, before we –

AVA   I told you there would be consequences.

YASMIN   Please, I just needed to see…I needed to know.

AVA   You lied to me.

YASMIN   No.

AVA   You said you were with me!

YASMIN   And I am.

AVA   Then help me destroy it!

YASMIN   But it's art!

AVA   More than that, it's a relic… You know what happened, what he did to us.

YASMIN   Yes and it sickens me but he's gone now! The art is separate from /the art – the artist

AVA   – the artist.

YASMIN   We don't have to destroy it. You are dealing with some horrific trauma and what you need is some professional –

AVA   Shut up.

YASMIN   Professional counselling and therapy.

AVA   No, shut up SHUT UP! Don't you try to twist this round to my – You said you were going to help me!

YASMIN   I am helping you!

AVA   You're drowning me! I am so tired. I am so fucking tired of carrying this alone! And when I ask someone for – can't you just take a fucking stand with me?

YASMIN I will do anything I can to help you.

AVA You... you... you you are so full of shit!

YASMIN Ava –

AVA You're a hypocrite! You say that I can trust you, then you go behind my back; you say you want to help, but you don't actually care about me at all.

YASMIN That's not true.

AVA You think you're some – some hot shit journalist but you're a failure, Yasmin! You can't admit it to yourself but you're a failure! A sad, deluded, failure!

YASMIN I don't think this helping.

AVA You've got that right.

AVA grabs the closest weapon she can find – a pair of fearsome-looking scissors.

YASMIN What are you doing?

AVA Out of the way.

YASMIN What?

AVA Go on, stand aside.

YASMIN No.

AVA I'm serious.

YASMIN You won't do it. You can't.

AVA advances closer towards YASMIN.

AVA You're sure of that, are you?

Pause.

YASMIN Very well. (*Steps aside.*) Go on then. I can't stop you. Go on. This is what you want, isn't it? Go on then, free yourself, Ava. (*AVA's grip tightens.*) I'm letting you do it. What are you waiting for? Come on! It's yours, after all, do what you need to. Slice it to pieces. It'd be so easy! Now's your chance! Do it!

AVA's grip loosens, she sinks.

AVA   No... please... please destroy it.

YASMIN   Give the scissors to me.

AVA considers... then hands them over.

YASMIN takes the scissors, and turns them over in her hands – she will not be using them.

YASMIN   Now, there's going to be no burning, no slashing up, none of that.

AVA   You said you were with me.

YASMIN   I only want what's best for you.

AVA   What did you... what did you see? When you finally got what you wanted, when you lifted the sheet, what did you see? What did you see!?

YASMIN   TRUTH! I saw truth. And it was exquisite. And beautiful. And terrible!

I saw the mind of a genius perfectly expressed. A masterpiece, Ava! That's what I saw.

AVA   Go to hell.

YASMIN   No one else knows what happened to you – apart from Rowan, but you two are hardly the image of sisterly love, right? I know your story and I can help.

AVA   Yes, my story... I decide what happens!

YASMIN   Christ, don't be so naïve! Now, you're going to listen. You're going to listen to me. This is so much bigger than you now.

YASMIN holds out her phone to AVA, showing her the recording.

AVA   You – !

YASMIN   This is what's going to happen. We are going to announce the discovery of *Scarlet Sunday*. You're going to sell it to whichever gallery has the deepest pockets.

AVA   So it was really all about the money?

YASMIN   What? You really think that's what I'm after? I don't give a shit about the money! Keep it all! Have you not listened to anything I've been saying? All I care about is the truth! I'm going to write this book, telling the story of what he did to you, and you're going to help me.

The whole world should know the truth, they have a right, Ava! *Scarlet Sunday* is integral to that truth. It's a work of genius, and one that people should see in all its beauty and terror. They will know the truth about the man who created it, and that truth may hurt them, but they can make their own minds up. That's how it should be.

All this tearing down and burning won't do anything but sweep his crimes under the carpet.

As for you? Sell the painting, sell this house, move far far away from here. Start a new life. Then maybe some good can finally come out of all this bad.

AVA   Sell *Scarlet Sunday*...it will be gone from here.

YASMIN   You never have to see it again. In fact, I can take it today for safe keeping until we're ready.

AVA   For so long...destroying it was the only way I could see out of this.

YASMIN   I know. But this is a better way. You've gone through so much. It's unimaginable. But that can all end now. I'll be there for you. I can look after you. A new life is possible. If you're with me?

AVA   I'm – I'm with you.

YASMIN   You've made the right choice. We don't need to rush into things but we'll need to discuss next steps, announcements, we'll need to start doing interviews for the book –

AVA   I just need it gone, as soon as possible.

YASMIN   I'll take care of it. I meant what I said, Ava, everyone will know your story, you have my word.

AVA   Okay.

YASMIN   I just have one question.

AVA   Yes.

YASMIN   If you don't mind?

AVA   What is it?

YASMIN   Why do you think he did it?

AVA   No one stopped him.

Pause.

YASMIN   I need a drink. Not gin, driving – plus it makes me depressed. Tea. Let's go downstairs, you can show me where the bits are and I'll make us some tea.

AVA   You want tea? In this heat?

YASMIN   Mmmm good point. Do you have lemonade?

AVA   I don't have lemonade.

YASMIN   No. Well, downstairs will be cooler at least.

AVA   Sure.

YASMIN   Come on then, let's get out of here.

They head towards the door. YASMIN leaves the pair of scissors on a table.

YASMIN   Everything is going to be fine now, Ava.

AVA   Yasmin?

YASMIN   Yes?

By this point YASMIN has exited through the door, while AVA is still standing just on the other side of the threshold, still in the studio.

AVA   I just wanted to say thank you.

YASMIN   You really don't need to thank me for anything.

AVA   I think I do. Thank you, Yasmin, for showing me exactly what I need to do.

Moving quickly, AVA closes the door in front of YASMIN. AVA takes a key from her pocket and locks the door.

YASMIN *(Off)* Ava? *(Knocks on the door.)* What are you doing? Ava, let me in.

Knocking more frantically.

With single-minded purpose, AVA walks towards 'Scarlet Sunday', picking up the scissors as she goes.

YASMIN   This isn't funny, Ava, let me in. What are you doing?

Birdsong. YASMIN hammers on the door.

YASMIN   Ava, Ava, stop, please stop! We can talk about this! Please! Stop! No! Ava, please let me in.

LET ME IN!!!

YASMIN hammers on the door harder.

AVA raises the scissors above her head. She breathes deeply, then brings the scissors down, slashing through the canvas. The room turns to red.

AVA slashes again, and again, tearing it to pieces. YASMIN howls, cries, pounds on the door.

YASMIN cries, AVA smiles.

Birdsong.

Lights down.

The End.

NEXT LESSON by Chris Woodley
ISBN 978-1-912430-19-2   £9.99

CARE TAKERS by Billy Cowan
9781910798-81-2   £9.99

THREE WOMEN by Matilda Velevitch
ISBN 978-1-912430-35-2   £9.99

PROJECT XXX by Kim Wiltshire & Paul Hine
ISBN 978-1-906582-55-5   £8.99

COMBUSTION by Asif Khan
ISBN 978-1-911501-91-6   £9.99

DIARY OF A HOUNSLOW GIRL by Ambreen Razia
ISBN 978-0-9536757-9-1   £8.99

SPLIT/MIXED by Ery Nzaramba
ISBN 978-1-911501-97-8   £10.99

THE TROUBLE WITH ASIAN MEN by Sudha Bhuchar, Kristine Landon-Smith and Louise Wallinger
ISBN 978-1-906582-41-8   £8.99

UNDER THEIR INFLUENCE by Wayne Buchanan
ISBN 978-0-9536757-5-3   £6.99

HARVEST by Manjula Padmanabhan
ISBN 978-0-9536757-7-7   £6.99

I HAVE BEFORE ME A REMARKABLE DOCUMENT by Sonja Linden
ISBN 978-0-9546912-3-3   £7.99

NEW SOUTH AFRICAN PLAYS ed. Charles J. Fourie
ISBN 978-0-9542330-1-3   £11.99

BLACK AND ASIAN PLAYS Anthology introduced by Afia Nkrumah
ISBN 978-0-9536757-4-6   £12.99

SIX PLAYS BY BLACK AND ASIAN WOMEN WRITERS ed. Kadija George
ISBN 978-0-9515877-2-0   £12.99

More great plays at:
www.aurorametro.com